SEX

ADVENT CALENDAR

Enjoy!

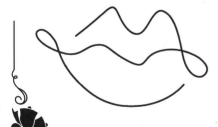

THIS VOUCHER ENTITLES YOU TO A :

HOT AND STEAMY SHOWER SEX

I LOVE YOU

STRATEGICALLY PLACED WHIPPED CREAM

I LOVE YOU

TERMS & CONDITIONS:
CAN BE REDEEMED ONLY ON WEEKENDS,
NOT WEEK DAYS. THE COUPON HOLDER
MUST BE IN THEIR OWN BED.
NON-TRANSFERABLE.

THIS VOUCHER ENTITLES YOU TO A :

LICK MY ??

I LOVE YOU

THIS VOUCHER ENTITLES YOU TO A :

NAKED CHEF

I LOVE YOU

DEC

5

THIS VOUCHER ENTITLES YOU TO A :

LET'S MAKE A MOVIE

I LOVE YOU

THIS VOUCHER ENTITLES YOU TO A :

QUICKIE (IN PULIC)

I LOVE YOU

THIS VOUCHER ENTITLES YOU TO A :

MORNING SEX

I LOVE YOU

TERMS & CONDITIONS:
CAN BE REDEEMED ONLY ON WEEKENDS,
NOT WEEK DAYS. THE COUPON HOLDER
MUST BE IN THEIR OWN BED.
NON-TRANSFERABLE.

THIS VOUCHER ENTITLES YOU TO A :

DAY TO SLEEP IN

I LOVE YOU

THIS VOUCHER ENTITLES YOU TO A :

ONE HOUR OF DIRTY TALK

I LOVE YOU

THIS VOUCHER ENTITLES YOU TO A :

VISIT THE 'TOY' STORE

I LOVE YOU

THIS VOUCHER ENTITLES YOU TO A :

ONE OUTING WITHOUT PANTIES

I LOVE YOU

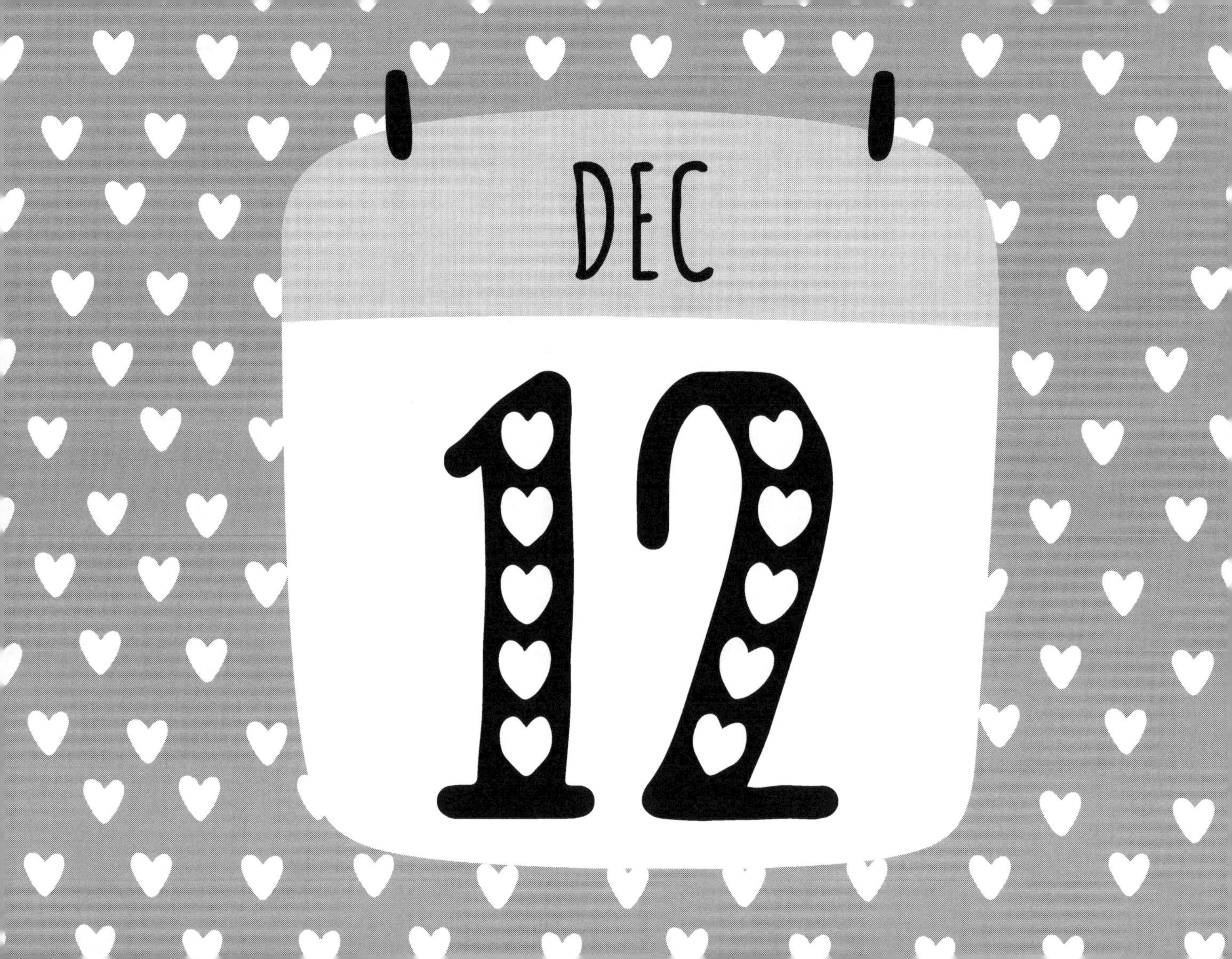
DEC
12

THIS VOUCHER ENTITLES YOU TO A :

BREAKFAST IN BED SERVED IN BODY

I LOVE YOU

TERMS & CONDITIONS:
CAN BE REDEEMED ONLY ON WEEKENDS,
NOT WEEK DAYS. THE COUPON HOLDER
MUST BE IN THEIR OWN BED.
NON-TRANSFERABLE.

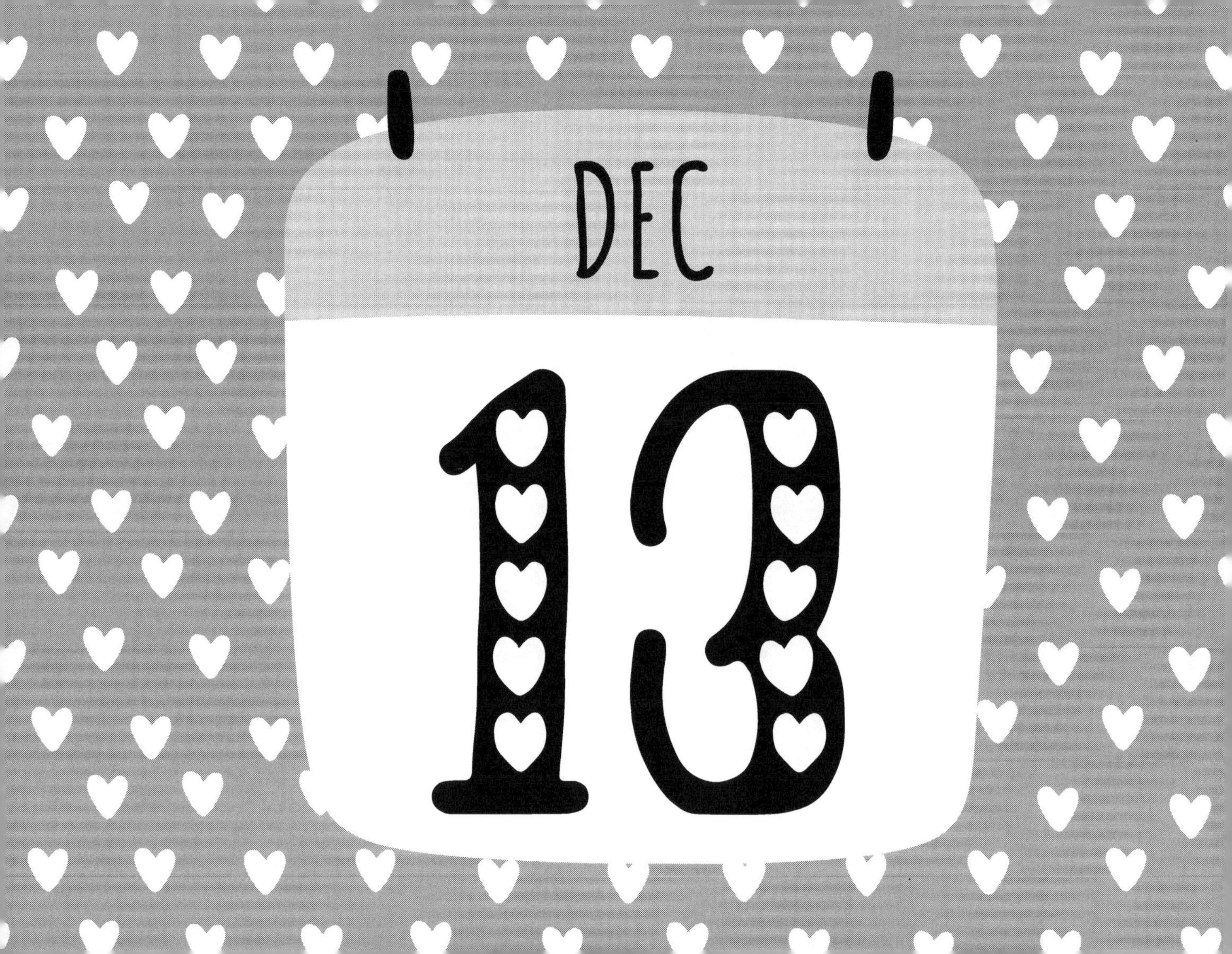
DEC
13

THIS VOUCHER ENTITLES YOU TO A :

SEX TOYS PLEASURE

I LOVE YOU

DEC
14

THIS VOUCHER ENTITLES YOU TO A:

OUTDOOR BLOWJOB

I LOVE YOU

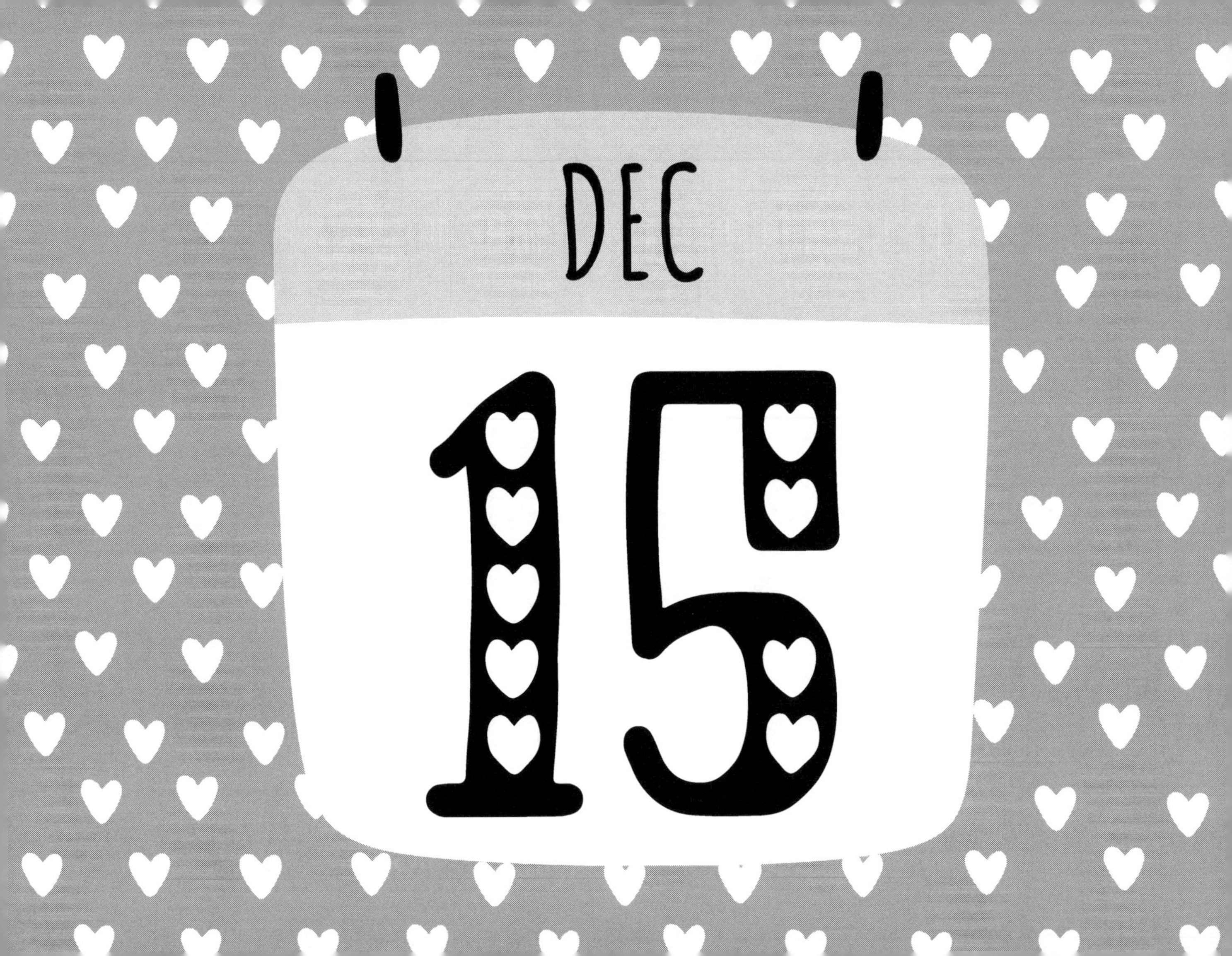
DEC
15

THIS VOUCHER ENTITLES YOU TO A :

KISS MY ??

I LOVE YOU

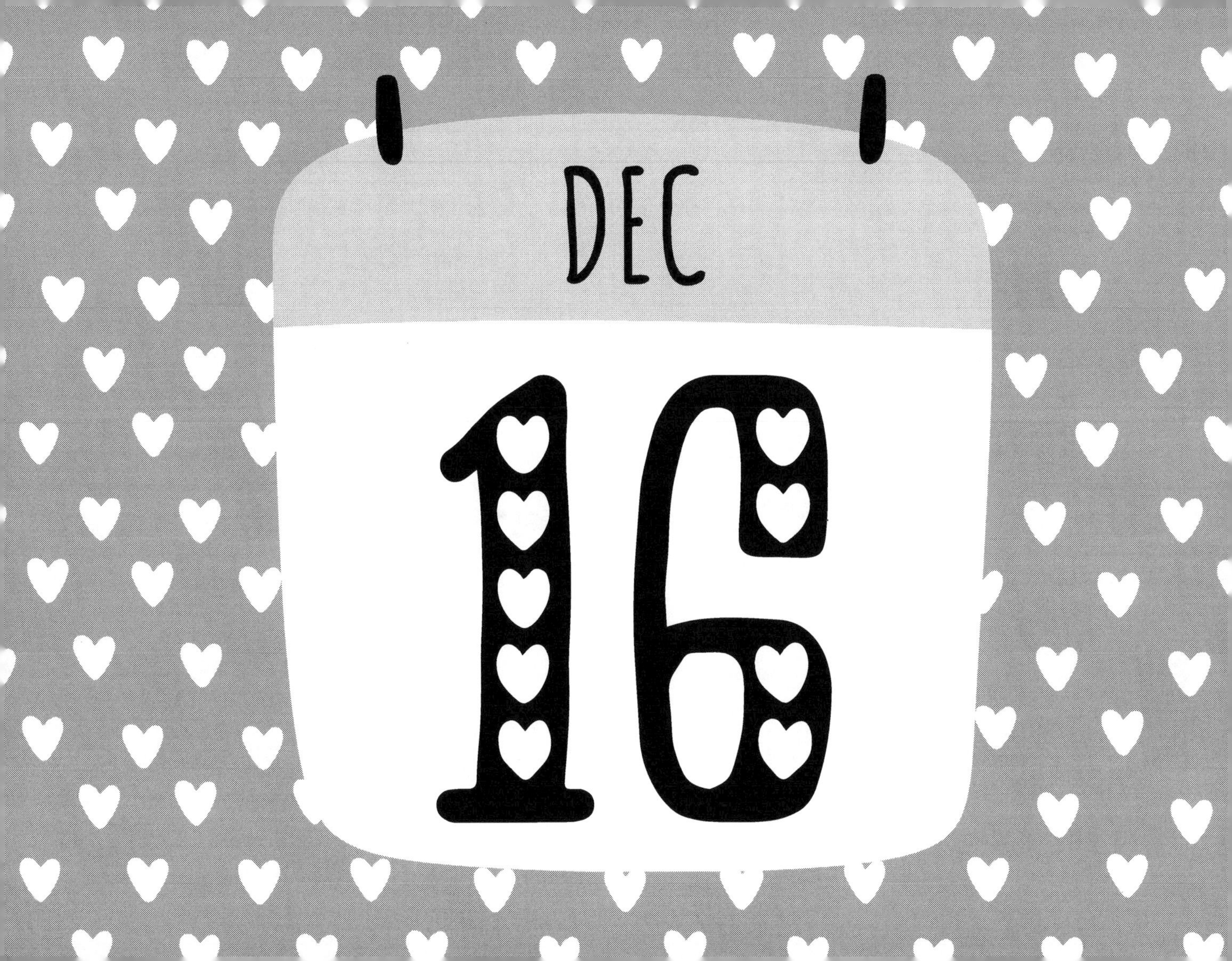
DEC
16

THIS VOUCHER ENTITLES YOU TO A :

LONGEST KISS EVER

I LOVE YOU

<u>TERMS & CONDITIONS:</u>
CAN BE REDEEMED ONLY ON WEEKENDS,
NOT WEEK DAYS. THE COUPON HOLDER
MUST BE IN THEIR OWN BED.
NON-TRANSFERABLE.

THIS VOUCHER ENTITLES YOU TO A :

USE FOR A NAUGHTY FREE WISH

I LOVE YOU

TERMS & CONDITIONS:
CAN BE REDEEMED ONLY ON WEEKENDS, NOT WEEK DAYS. THE COUPON HOLDER MUST BE IN THEIR OWN BED. NON-TRANSFERABLE.

THIS VOUCHER ENTITLES YOU TO A :

CHOICE OF LOCATION FOR WHERE WE HAVE SEX

I LOVE YOU

DEC
19

THIS VOUCHER ENTITLES YOU TO A :

FOOTJOB

I LOVE YOU

THIS VOUCHER ENTITLES YOU TO A :

A NIGHT AT A HOTEL

I LOVE YOU

DEC

21

THIS VOUCHER ENTITLES YOU TO A:

69 SESSSION

I LOVE YOU

TERMS & CONDITIONS:
CAN BE REDEEMED ONLY ON WEEKENDS,
NOT WEEK DAYS. THE COUPON HOLDER
MUST BE IN THEIR OWN BED.
NON-TRANSFERABLE.

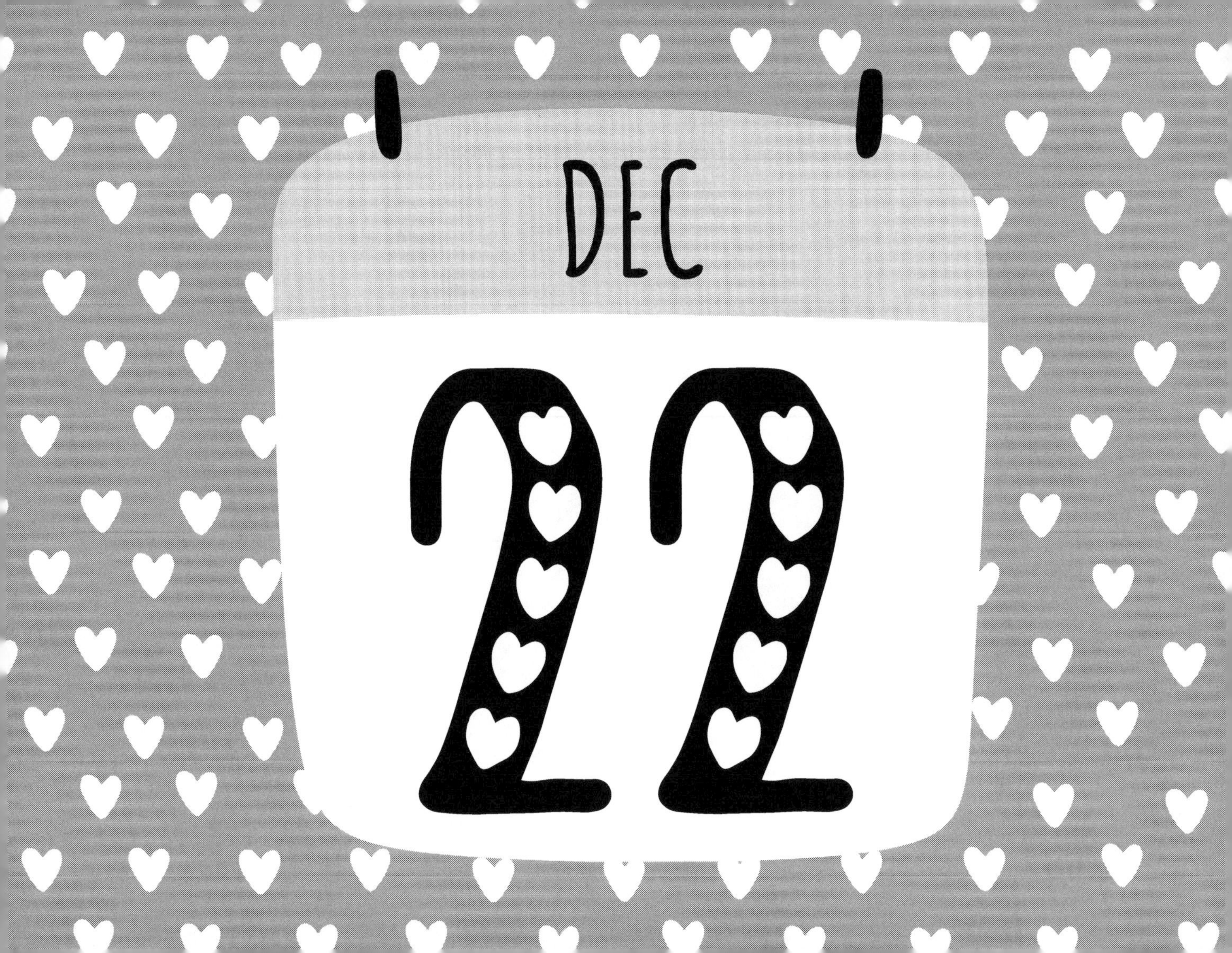
DEC
22

THIS VOUCHER ENTITLES YOU TO A :

BLINDFOLD FUN

I LOVE YOU

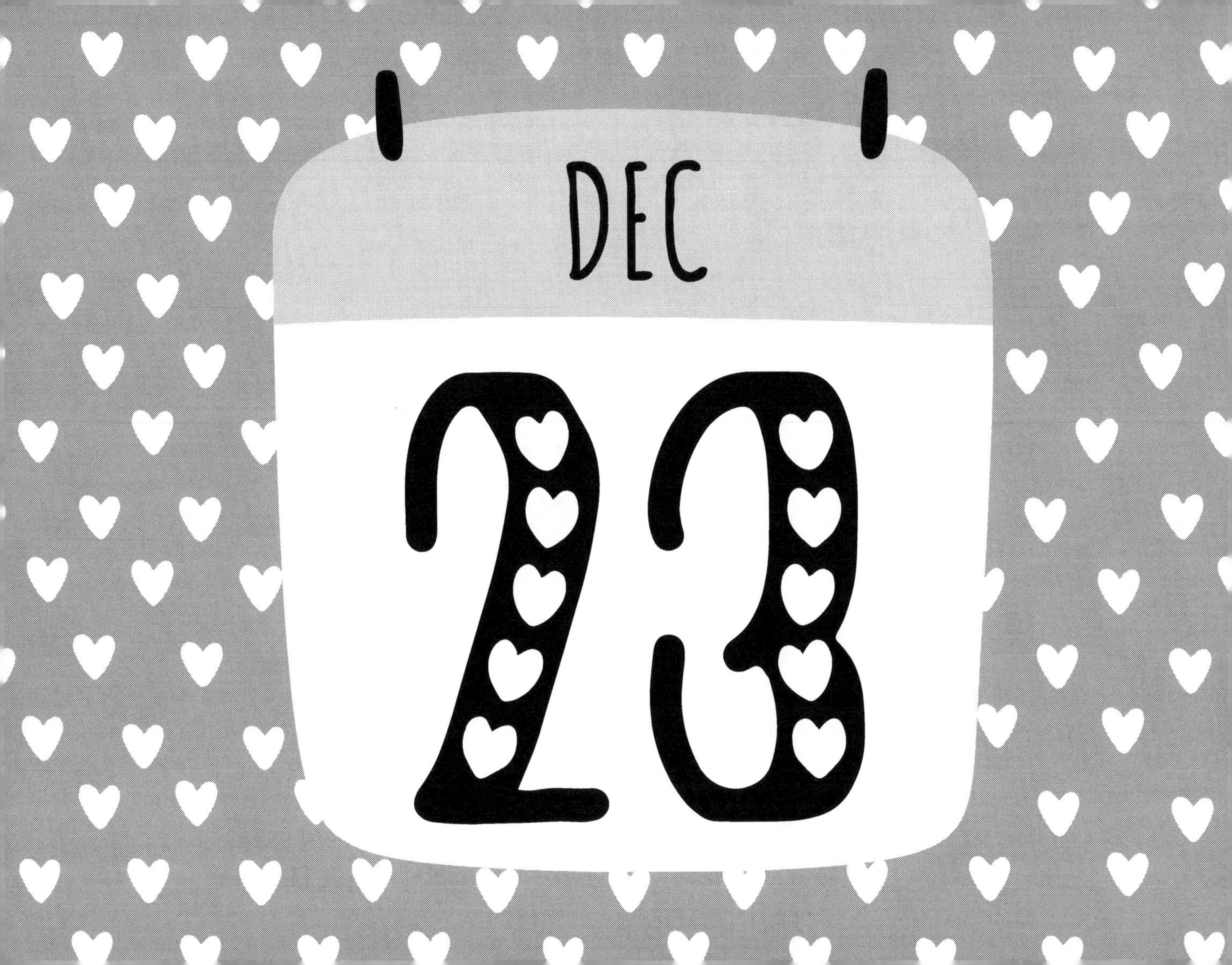
DEC
23

THIS VOUCHER ENTITLES YOU TO A:

ANAL PLAY

I LOVE YOU

THIS VOUCHER ENTITLES YOU TO A :

tie me up

I LOVE YOU

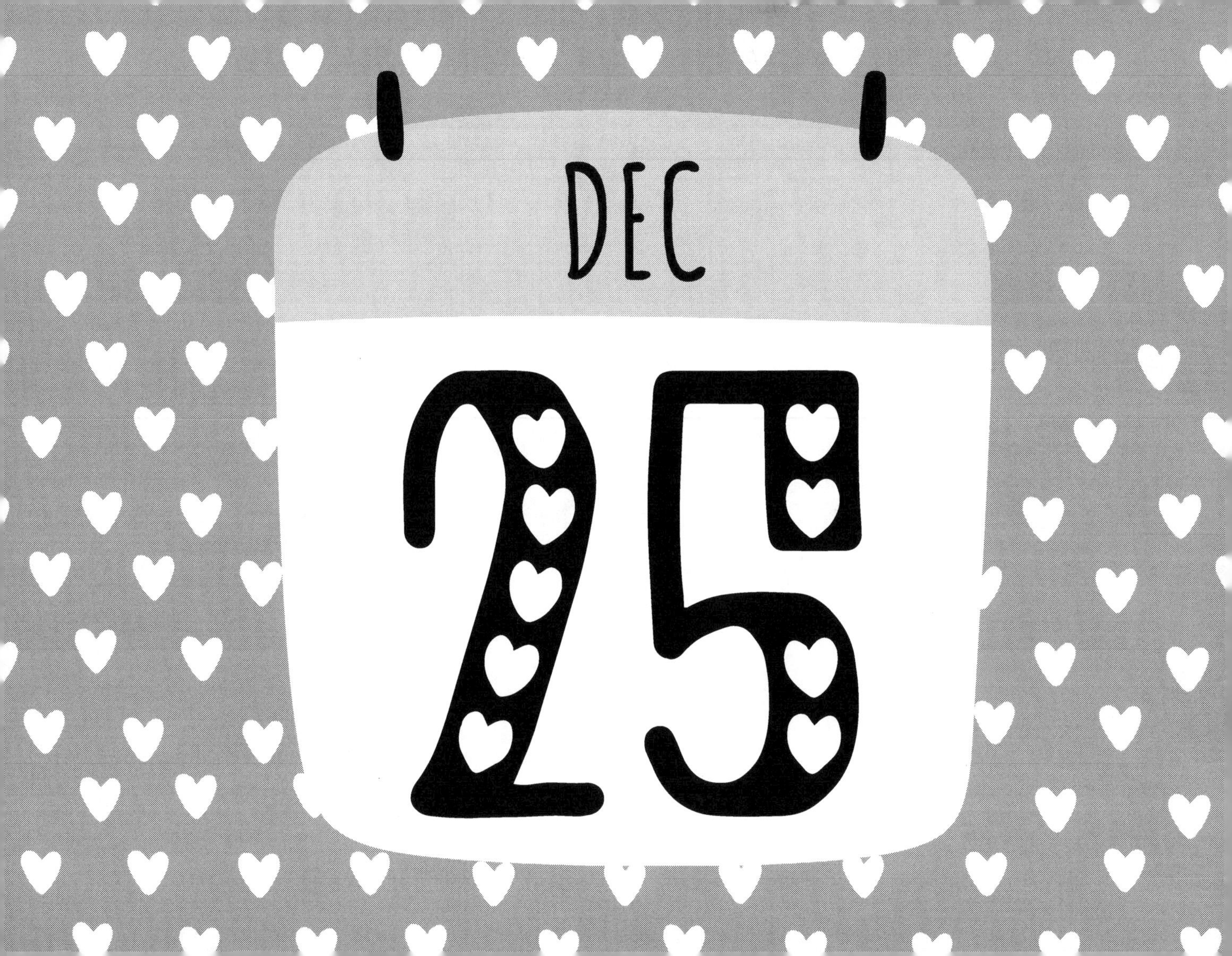
DEC
25

THIS VOUCHER ENTITLES YOU TO A :

LICK NIPPLES

I LOVE YOU

Made in United States
Troutdale, OR
12/21/2023

16326991R00031